THE FEARS

ALSO BY KEVIN PRUFER

POETRY

The Art of Fiction

I Had Wanted a Happier Ending

How He Loved Them

Churches

In a Beautiful Country

National Anthem

Fallen from a Chariot

The Finger Bone

Strange Wood

AS EDITOR

Jean Ross Justice: On the Life and Work of an American Master
(with Ryan Bollenbach)

World'd Too Much: The Selected Poetry of Russell Atkins
(with Robert E. McDonough)

Into English: Poems, Translations, Commentaries (with Martha Collins)

Literary Publishing in the Twenty-First Century
(with Travis Kurowski and Wayne Miller)

Catherine Breese Davis: On the Life and Work of an American Master
(with Martha Collins and Martin Rock)

Russell Atkins: On the Life and Work of an American Master
(with Michael Dumanis)

Until Everything Is Continuous Again: American Poets on the Recent Work of W.S. Merwin (with Jonathan Weinert)

Dunstan Thompson: On the Life and Work of a Lost American Master
(with D.A. Powell)

New European Poets (with Wayne Miller)

Dark Horses: Poets on Overlooked Poems (with Joy Katz)

The New Young American Poets

THE FEARS

KEVIN PRUFER

COPPER CANYON PRESS

PORT TOWNSEND, WASHINGTON

Cover art: Bronze portrait of young athlete recovered from the square peristyle of the Villa dei Papyri in the 1754 excavations, one of a pair, inv. no 5626, Naples, National Archaeological Museum. Photo credit: Mary Harrsch (CC BY-SA 4.0).

Copper Canyon Press is in residence at Fort Worden State Park in Port Townsend, Washington, under the auspices of Centrum. Centrum is a gathering place for artists and creative thinkers from around the world, students of all ages and backgrounds, and audiences seeking extraordinary cultural enrichment.

LIBRARY OF CONGRESS CATALOGING-IN-PUBLICATION DATA
Names: Prufer, Kevin, author.
Title: The fears / Kevin Prufer.
Description: Port Townsend, Washington : Copper Canyon Press, [2023]
Identifiers: LCCN 2023021344 (print) | LCCN 2023021345 (ebook) |
    ISBN 9781556596643 (paperback) | ISBN 9781619322813 (epub)
Subjects: LCGFT: Poetry.
Classification: LCC PS3566.R814 F43 2023 (print) |
    LCC PS3566.R814 (ebook) | DDC 811/.54—dc23/eng/20230522
LC record available at https://lccn.loc.gov/2023021344
LC ebook record available at https://lccn.loc.gov/2023021345

9 8 7 6 5 4 3 2 FIRST PRINTING

COPPER CANYON PRESS

Post Office Box 271
Port Townsend, Washington 98368
www.coppercanyonpress.org

ACKNOWLEDGMENTS

These poems originally appeared in *The Adroit Journal, AGNI, The American Poetry Review, Bennington Review, Colorado Review, Crazyhorse, The Hudson Review, The Louisville Review, The Massachusetts Review, New England Review, Paperbag, Poetry International, Plume, Puerto del Sol, Red Canary, The Southern Review, Tin House,* and *Waxwing*.

"In This Way" was published in *Voices Amidst the Virus: Poets Respond to the Pandemic,* edited by Eileen Cleary and Christine Jones (Lily Poetry Review Books).

"A Dog Barking into the Night" and "W.H. Auden's 'The Fall of Rome'" first appeared in the limited-edition chapbook *I Had Wanted a Happier Ending,* published by Sting & Honey Press.

Thanks to Stephen Frech for his design and editorial acumen.

Thanks also to Erin Belieu, Noah Blaustein, Teresa Cader, and Jonathan Weinert for help and encouragement along the way.

for Wayne Miller and Martha Collins, always my first readers

CONTENTS

ONE

5 A Dog Barking into the Night

9 A Body of Work

10 A History of My Schooling

12 Finger

16 The Cities, the Armies

19 Condominiums

TWO

23 W.H. Auden's "The Fall of Rome"

27 Increasingly Improbable

31 Ants

33 Ars Poetica

35 The Greek Gods

38 The Fears

THREE

43 Election Night

46 In This Way

49 Extended Metaphor for Bad Government

51 The Last of Diocletian

53 My Jug of Poison

55 Late Empires

FOUR

59   A Distant Row of Black Pines

64   Cannibalism

66   The Time Machine

71   Absences

75   Anesthesia

78   Automotive

83   *About the Author*

THE FEARS

ONE

A Dog Barking into the Night

Creon's error is remarkable
when viewed as confusion

                    about the proper placement
of the living and the dead,

                    for Antigone, whom he seals
in a cave, is a vital young woman and so
belongs in the sun.

                    It is her brother,
already dead on the sunlit battlefield,

                              who requires a tomb.

+

It makes sense, therefore,

                    that Antigone hangs herself,
death being the circumstance
her placement demands.

                    Thus, Creon creates
from nothing

                    a situation that requires
two tombs.

                    It's like the saddest time
of my life.

                    Let me explain:

+

One evening years ago

                    in Cleveland,
my brother and I

                    stood on his front porch smoking.
Our father was in the hospital

                              dying.

All night long,

                    a chained dog whimpered into the frozen night.

It isn't right, my brother said,

                          to keep a dog

chained up like that.

                    I nodded and took another drag,

smoke filling my lungs

                  as a thought

fills the mind.

               And then we went inside.

+

The next morning, as I got in my car,

ready to drive to the hospital,

                     I found that dog

frozen by the chain-link fence.

                       Snow had crusted

over his chain. It wasn't right,

+

                    of course. The dog

belonged inside. It was an error

of placement.

               My father wasting away in his hospital bed—

at that point in his illness,

                    he became an animal, too,

+

his hands,

           I'm not kidding,

                  looked like claws

curved around the remote control.

                     I will not forget how,

because he could not get out of bed,

and the nurses had grown
complacent,
         I held his cock in my hand
while he pissed into a dirty drinking glass.
                              Thank you,
he said when he was through.

+

               And in that moment,
I could not remember him
                    the way I knew he'd once been,
a man, a human being,
                    more than the accumulation
of the failures
               of a dying animal body.
Hospitals

+

         do this to you. The rattle of pill carts,
the nurses and their iPads.
                         I was teaching a class
on Greek drama
               and had come to that point in *Antigone*
where Creon realizes his error,
                              where, too late,
he corrects his mistake,
burying Antigone's brother
                         properly. By then, she has hanged
herself,
         making her placement in the cave abruptly
perfect.

+

I had wanted a happier ending
for my father,
                sitting by his bedside,
making notes in the margins
of my book.
                At the back of the cancer ward,
the private elevator
                        was large enough for a gurney.
I imagined it went right down
                        a dark throat
to a basement.

+

                I held his claw and read.
Soon, my brother would visit,
still angry about his neighbor's dog.
                                When the nurse asked
if we needed anything,
I didn't even look up from my book.
                                No,
I told her. My father was asleep.
                                The dog was dead.
Antigone was a beautiful fifteen-year-old girl,
and then she was,
                like her brother,
like all of us, eventually,
                        nowhere.

A Body of Work

One comes, eventually, to the realization
that one will leave behind only
a body of work that will grow increasingly
unintelligible to each new generation. A trace
will remain spread across the vast
internet much the way certain particles
inhabit the emptiness of deep space—negligibly,
though perhaps measurably. I, for instance,
am childless and, therefore, most likely
will die alone, my nest feathered
with yellowing poems. One comes, eventually,
to the knowledge that one's children
are increasingly unintelligible, being yellowing
poems spread across the emptiness of deep space—
negligible, though they once seemed, in their way,
to breathe. For instance, I am alive, right here,
in the middle of my poem, having had, perhaps,
too much to drink. One comes, eventually,
to the certainty that one's body of work
is nothing like another man's progeny, being
made of language, which can only veer
toward emptiness as years become empty space.
For instance, hello? I am calling out to you,
folded here between the pages
of generations. You don't know me, but once
I was particulate and alive. Now what am I?

A History of My Schooling

If you don't leave a close study of antiquity
with an appreciation for the cheapness
                                                of human life
then you are a fool,
                        I used to think.

Armies swept across Illyria
like spilled paint
                spreading over linoleum

one afternoon back then
when you sat on the floor
                                laughing in the windowlight
because really
                wasn't it too ridiculous,
all those dead generals in my books
while you just wanted
                                to paint the damned kitchen?
Your T-shirt was speckled with violet,
and the wet roller
                glistened in your hand.

The armies
                swept across Illyria in their glittering
breastplates. That century,
                                every pretender to the throne
wound up in a bathtub
                                full of his own blood. Not
really. But that's how it felt to me,
                                having to memorize
the stories of other people's troubles
for Thursday's exam

while you whom I once loved,

                       having stumbled

coming down the ladder,

knocked over the paint can.

                  Carnage

slid over the linoleum and

what else was there to do

but close my book

and sit beside you on the floor

                        in the late afternoon light

while the Parthians

did something

          I couldn't quite remember

to an emperor whose name

                  I didn't recall

and you dipped your index finger

into the spreading violet

                and on my face

made war paint?

Finger

Remember how we hid in the college museum
until that old woman turned off the lights

and locked us in?

Then we camped out on the floor
among musty artifacts
and drank ourselves into hilarity.

You said we should take that old mummy out of his box
so he could join us.

He was so light,

like papier-mâché.

I propped him against the wall,
and when I tried to wedge a cigarette into his hand

a single finger broke off,
slipping through the linen

into my palm.

+

In those days,
I wanted to immortalize myself

in the pages of a novel
about a brilliant young man

who left his home in Cleveland
and did what?

I was still discovering
the plot. I smoked

and typed, then deleted what I typed.
It would be a mystery—

a body discovered strangled

among unspooled film reels

                in the back of an art-house theater—

+

And how you laughed when I leaped back,
the mummy's desiccated black finger
˙skittering across the floor.

How you held that finger like a half-smoked cigar
and waggled it at me. You were such
a hilarious failure,

Groucho Marx in the dark museum, lifting that finger
to your lips—

          you didn't care about anything,

+

you who would die

             jogging in a public park
among pigeons and ice-cream vendors
one evening later that June.

             Your sister
was already dead, head through a windshield.
Your father, too. It was a family

              tradition, you said,
holding that mummy's finger and laughing.
The mummy,

        also thralled in death,
leaned against the wall,

           ghostlit by streetlights—

+

The strangled girl among the unspooled reels
stared blankly

        at the ceiling fan that rustled the papers

on the little desk in the corner.
                              A single tear
dried on her cheek. *What was a life,*
                              I wrote,
but an infinitely replayable film?—

+

or some such nonsense.
                              I wanted to be
an important writer
                    and to be, therefore, immortal.

You were taking apart a suit of armor;
then you were kissing the marble head
                              of some dead emperor.

The mummy stayed lost
                    in his dream.
Someone had cared for him once.
Someone had rubbed his skin with ochre and resin,
then extracted his brain
                    lovingly through the nostrils.

+

We slept on the floor
having drunk
              far too much, our candles
gone out.
          When I woke, there you were
at the window
              looking over the lamplit
dead campus.

+

We packed the mummy back into his case
and, at dawn, slipped out of the museum

and disappeared
                        into our futures.

My novel would remain unfinished
                                    forever.

I've got that finger in a box on my writing desk.
Its black skin
                    has long since flaked away.
It looks like ivory.

My thumb has polished the bone.

The Cities, the Armies

In the bright days of ancient Rome
when a child was born
                    unwanted
her father might choose *exposure,*
which meant
               he might abandon the infant
in the forest
              where eventually
she would no longer be
                  a burden
to the family.

+

              For years, I tried
to understand the mind
                  that could be right
with this:
          a child in the leaves
crying into the night,
                the hungry wolves.
I could not
         understand it.
                    But there it was
in the history books—

+

The Romans
            have spoken to me over the centuries
and I have listened
              carefully,
and loved them more than I have loved
even my friends.

They whisper
into my ear,
                and I write down
every word they say,
                    and have made a career of it,

+

made a convenience of them.
                        What excites me most
is their apparent familiarity
                    that doesn't quite conceal
their foreignness. They are
                    a foreign
mind. An alien

+

                mind, they who could expose
a child
        so easily
                and thus make resonant the stories
of Moses,
            of Romulus and Remus, of Oedipus or Hercules,
fuck,

+

    I have lived fifty years and hope
I have done as little harm
                        as possible, though I
doubt it.
            My mother inherited her mother's
senility,
            by which I mean she loses her glasses
all the time

and probably will eventually forget

who I am.

+

           I do not want forgetfulness

                        for myself,

though I suppose in a broader sense

                        it might be a mercy

to forget who we once were.

                  These days, she reads

the same book over and over,

                and seems happy

with that.

+

           It is a book I gave her

                    about the many empires

that preceded us.

             Listen to this, she keeps saying.

Can you imagine

             the armies? Can you imagine the cities

those people once built?

Condominiums

What inspired the emperor Constantine
to murder his own son
                        and later
to have his name erased from monuments?

No one knows. Nevertheless,
Constantine was a benevolent ruler,
if you can believe
                    Church historians.

Late last night,
walking through the contagious city,
I came upon my demolished
high school.
                    Just like that,
they'd torn it down. Barbarians.

Once I'd sat in a tight desk
while an old nun lied
about American history.

Now it was a pile
                        of brick and glass.
A yellow bulldozer dozed
                            in the corner,
a fat tyrant.
                The rumble
of commerce was continuous
from the nearby highway.
How I love you,
                    America. You are so
forgetful. Constantine

ruled for decades
after his forgotten son's demise
and died happy in Nicomedia.

We should murder history
to make room
                for history.
No, I told myself. For truth.
No.
        Condominiums.

TWO

W.H. Auden's "The Fall of Rome"

In the final lines of his great poem "The Fall of Rome,"
Auden describes
           not the facts
of the late Empire's fall,
               but distant herds of reindeer
moving quickly and silently
across vast expanses of golden moss.
                  We don't know
where those herds are,
              only that they seem impossibly
far from the troubles of men,
                not mindless but
beyond mind,
          uncountable, twilit, inhuman,
unconcerned with the failures of empires.

+

So the human mind—
            my mind—
tries to concur,
          but the gap is too great. I cannot move
from mundanity to vastness
              to the erasure of the self
into vastness—

+

         though I once stood in my front yard
and with a kind of finality
             understood that one day I would die.
I was ten years old.
         We had apple trees then, and the wind
riffled through them.

The cat slept on the porch. The sunlight was
honey. You will die,
                                        you will die, you will die—it was the only
accounting
                    I could give myself,
a vastness, thrilling,
                                        an acknowledgment

+

of the cancellation physicists say
existed
                    outside the bubble of the young
expanding universe.
                                        What was on the other side
of that skin?
                    Nothing was.
                                        Zero was.
Death was.
                    Herds of reindeer traversing golden moss—

+

What I'm talking about here is the thrill
                                                        of terror.
Years later,
                    looking out the window as a Mexican gardener
pushed his wheelbarrow past students
throwing Frisbees on the quad
                                        while my professor
went on about the failures of Domitian,
                                                        I felt it again,
a certainty
                    that words weren't
imperfect mirrors reflecting reality,
                                        but they created

a reality out of
　　　　　　　　　nothing. A scrim
concealing emptiness. You will die,
　　　　　　　　　　　　　　you will die,
my mind told my body that was, in fact,
already at work on its own demise.

+

　　　　　　　　　　　　　　I am tired of the idea
that art must assert the identity of the artist
against the vastness of immediate social forces
when a more pressing problem
　　　　　　　　　　　　might be what my friend
Reginald called the experience of being *no one at all* ...

+

existing, however contingently, outside the shackles
of identity and definition.
　　　　　　　　　That is the destination
we are all approaching,
　　　　　　　　　and I want
to understand it
　　　　　　　before I get there.
I suppose

+

　　　　　　Reginald understands it now, having died
fifteen years ago
　　　　　　　　in Pensacola. We talked on the phone a lot
in his last days.
　　　　　　　He spoke quickly,
as if he wanted to communicate many ideas
before he forgot them all,
　　　　　　　　　as if he didn't have enough time. I cradled

the phone against my shoulder,

                stirring a pot of stew

while the CD player played the Ramones

                and Mary

parked her Toyota on the snow-covered driveway

+

and Reginald went on about how his poetry

could never quite exactly communicate

every nuance

        of a particular experience

perfectly—

+

        Now he is altogether

elsewhere,

        not outside the expanding universe, but not in it,

either.

      At any rate, he cannot

              explain his position.

And those reindeer I keep mentioning

+

and their never-ending tundra,

             unconcerned with us,

silent, unlocatable—

          The mind has motion, tides, breezes.

The world, too.

        The reindeer are moving.

                I can't

get closer to death

        than that.

Increasingly Improbable

What if
      I never transform
from alive
       to dead,
my heart
      never caves
and the internet
        of my brain
extends indefinitely;
          what if, instead of dying,
I grow merely
      increasingly
improbable,
     my consciousness

+

never snuffed,
     its continued existence
contingent upon
      the more and more unlikely
circumstances that keep me
        alive?
Thus my consciousness
persists
    while the world becomes stranger
to accommodate it,

the world's
eventual complete
      weirdness
essential to what keeps me
       alive.

+

Wouldn't that be something?

+

When I was a teenager
and only just awakening
to the fact
        of death,
that was the kind of fantasy
                        I indulged in—stories
of a perpetually living being
inhabiting an increasingly
                unlikely world
that existed only to keep consciousness alive,

+

as if the world cared that much for anyone.
In my heart
        I knew it didn't.
Of course
        not.

+

For many years,
        I had a cat, Nightingale.
Most evenings, I lay in bed
            and read. Nightingale
lay on my chest and purred thoughtlessly.
She was so
        predictable,
           until one evening,
she didn't appear at the porch.

The next day, too.

After a while,
    I realized Nightingale
must be dead.

+

It's hard to describe
the space I will once have filled.
        Recently,
I drove past my childhood home.

Back then, it was yellow.
       Now it is deep blue.

Will I be the minute space
between those coats of paint,
      narrow
and obliterated?
     I have written poems

+

and uploaded them
     to the mind of Literature.

If they hover in probable silence,
I hope it is the silence of thought

+

and not negation.
     Once, long ago,
Nightingale descended
those porch stairs
     and disappeared grayly
into the night.

Each evening, I stood on the porch
and called into darkness,

                              rattling food in her bowl.

Then, every morning,
                       I descended
those same steps
                  and got in the car
as if nothing
had changed for me,
                   as if nothing were
missing,

+

exactly as I still do every day,
as I will do tomorrow
                   and maybe
thousands of times after that
into the future.

Ants

The most insignificant emperors
are of more historical importance
than I will ever be.
                    Consider Galba,
who reigned seven months,
                                    done in
by Otho, who lasted three.
                            The imperial
succession,

+

            like the long list of Nobel laureates,
is mostly obscure,
which is to say
                that I should find in them
points of self-identification,
being, myself,

+

            totally obscure. That
I haven't—that I laughed at those
Swedish myopics
                who skipped Borges
and offered us, instead,
                            someone called
Laxness—is evidence
                        that I have failed
to consider my own
eventual complete
                    negation,

+

though earlier today
      I found the cat's bowl
overrun with sugar ants.
     The cat,
who understood his place,
       would have none of it,
but sat beneath the deck furniture
eyeing me meanly,

+

     and in that second,
my mind reached back to
those whose names come down to us
        barely,
the way distant astral bodies
       appear as the tiniest pixels
on an observatory's computer screen,

+

faint echoes within time.
      Moments earlier,
I had been enthusiastically
typing into my computer
      my most intimate history
and now
   I held this cat-food bowl in my hand
and it was swarming with ants.
       Like a god,
I took that bowl to the sink
and washed it.

Ars Poetica

The skull admits no light.
The brain turns blackly on its stem.
Strange full lily. Moonless night.
The brain in its black pond. Prehistoric
fish. Translucent pin teeth.
The skull admits
no light. A poem
could show the shifting
of such a brain at work
on what? It rocks on its stem
when wind unsettles the tall grasses,
then skitters over the pond's
black surface. No words
yet. Another breeze. We are
resting here
for a little while in the lightless
skull. It's okay to be silent.
Such cruelties in the world.
Just be silent,
says the night heron
observing from the reeds.
Be silent, says the raft the children
made from a barn door.
Quiet, says the empty
gravel road. Beyond that line of trees,
a window glows. There you are
in front of your blue screen,
unmoving. Silent cruelties.
It's okay. Write nothing
at all. Your brain is in the pond,
under a sky of bone.
So quiet down here
in the warm water.

High above, a quick bat
has a white moth in its teeth.

The Greek Gods

Because they are immortal,

                     time does not pass for them

the way it does for us. Instead,

it unravels

           endlessly.

Therefore, unlike yours,

a god's life resists

           summary.

+

It may be more accurate to say

the ancient Greeks believed in *immortal*

                   forces—

the force of sexual desire,

of chastity, or war, or ocean.

               Poseidon, for instance:

+

Why, you might ask,

                does he terrorize Odysseus?

Because Odysseus blinded his son,

the Cyclops?

          Or because the ocean is *in fact*

unforgiving

          and terrifying.

+

That I love you

          is a fact. (Sappho would have said

that Aphrodite set my veins

              on fire.) But here you are

in the hospital

and when your heart fibrillates,
the machine beeps

+

incessantly. It's always
                    beeping. The nurses,
like the distant gods,
                    don't care,
hard at work on word search puzzles
in their brightly lit stations,

+

so I've learned not to be alarmed, either.
I just hit the button that says
                    "reset"
and get back to my book

+

                    about the Greek gods
and their vast removal from us.
                    The Christian desire
to whisper into the ear of Jesus
                    and have him whisper back
makes sense
          among the dying,

+

but Greek loneliness
               seems closer to explaining
the forces that brought us here
               and make me wander
the hospital skybridges
               late at night,

watching that same McDonald's blinking

                      into darkness.

+

Listen: Once

          you were vibrant, you were really
alive. And now you are

              intubated. Now you are
nosocomial. But I still love you.

+

Otherwise I wouldn't be packing up my things
to head home for a few hours' sleep,

                  maybe get my grade book
in order

      before driving that same route back here
in the morning,

+

        a route that, next year, when
for some reason I happen to take it,

              might create
within me

      the memory of those long days
visiting you here

         among the still alive.

The Fears

He had become fascinated by the way
excellent poems sometimes failed to hold together
in ways he expected them to.
                                    That is,
a poem, like a great mind at work
on an unsolvable problem,
                                    might by necessity
meander, might come up against
                                    a bad image or a wrong idea,
might turn down a particularly dark passage—
a frightening passage—
                    only to be confronted
by an unexpected crumbling

fountain in the form of a satyr
out of scale beside a wild swan
at the center of a small, unpopulated courtyard
late on a windy night
                    in an unfamiliar town,

and he realized, of course,
that this was not at all
                    what the mind had sought—
or so he imagined,
                    looking at the mess of his own writing
which, indeed, meandered
                    into unsettling courtyards.

On the other side of the window,
sleet glittered briefly as it passed beneath the streetlamps
before stippling the wet road,

and tree branches that only seemed dead
swayed in the wind,

tapped against his window now and then,

the cold outside speaking in strange unison,
the tires cutting the sleet, the slap of a flag
against its pole—
                    it all seemed to say at once,
You don't really matter,
which was
            exactly the fear that had distracted him
at the beginning of this poem. *You're going to vanish,*
he said quietly to himself,
                            the sentiment having bubbled up
just perfectly,
                a perfect, impossible little thought.

Yet he knew the world to be an ordered system.

Once the invisible hand of God set it in motion,
every occurrence was part of a vast
                        unfolding
of events, each predicated on events that preceded it.
Nothing,
        he knew, was unpredictable, but the limits
of his data prevented him from knowing.
That he would die was a certainty,
                            but his mind
was too small. And what did it mean,
to *matter*?
            And why should he have fears? The sleet
caught the streetlamp's glare like fleeting insects.
So quick.
        Uncountable. It made sense
to live in agreement with the events
unfolding around him.
                    He should focus
on the poem he was writing,

that one with the fountain,

                        the satyr and the swan,

that strange courtyard one hot summer night

empty of citizenry—it was

                  very late—

an August rain coming on now,

fat hot drops staining the paving stones

                              beside the abandoned

café tables,

           and far away the rumbling of a train,

well lit, in each window

                  a traveler reading a newspaper

or looking into a blue, glowing screen,

                        the train easing

through the ancient countryside,

                    into the blackness

of nightfall, Etruscan, unknowable,

               sleet

outside his own window,

            he wasn't afraid now,

he was a part of the performance

into which, a hundred years ago, Rilke wrote,

I have taken action against fear.

                I sat up the whole night

and wrote; and now I am as thoroughly tired

as after a long walk in the fields at Ulsgaard.

Those words came down to him,

              talked to him

as he poured himself another drink

               that winter night

not many years ago

         when he began to write this poem.

THREE

Election Night

Are you ready?
              I nodded. She slid the needle in
and the sick cat,
                    who only a moment before had tried to
leap to the floor,
                  closed his eyes and exhaled. *And*
that's it, she said
                  a little too brightly, pulling the needle out.
That's it? I asked.
                 That's all there is to it.

+

The syringe going in
                 and then the pressure
when the vet pressed the plunger,
                     familiar,
then unfamiliar, a sort of sparkling
                      in the corners
of the cat's eyes
              like fireflies in the darkening backyard—
and then the sparkling
                grew thick and filled the air,
handfuls of black
          glitter—

+

Hours earlier, after I had voted, I found the dog
had strewn garbage over the kitchen floor,
                    the TV on
loud—a commercial for pharmaceuticals.
                  The cat was
still alive at the vet's.

All I wanted was to lie on the sofa
and read my book,
        The Life of Nero,
                and not think about the election

+

while the cat suffered in his cube and the dog
eyed me hungrily,
         and Piso, conspirator against Nero,
plotted his assassination in dark chambers,
because it seemed the only right option,
Rome in disarray,
         the treasury plundered, Nero's own mother ordered
murdered.
       We must become a republic
again, Piso declared grandly,
           then, betrayed by spies,
succeeded only in entrapping
        himself.

+

And later I sat on the sofa drinking wine while the returns
came in
      and the body of my cat became ashes at the vet's,

and Piso cut his wrists
in the courtyard behind his villa
         while his wife
stroked his sun-dappled hair,
       and he exhaled one last time.

+

It began as a kind of sparkling,
just out of the range of vision,

              and then it slowly filled
the entire field,
           until all I could see was a curtain
of glitter,
       behind which the new engines of power
worked—

+

So many fireflies while the TV played the terrible news,
and my cat no longer sat beside me
                purring,
And *That's it,*
         a voice said from somewhere—
the TV? Blackness behind the trees,

the dog barking into the darkness,
the neighborhood enclosed in night.
              That's it? I asked
the empty room, encased
in sheets of dark glitter,
         of history and sadness,
senseless, now,
       the election decided. *That's all
there is to it,*
      the voice explained.

In This Way

There probably was a Trojan War,
a skirmish between small
rival towns,
           but we receive
only its echoes
                  in literature. Facts about the battle
are obscure,
          endlessly transformed
by the Greek tragedians.
               In this way,
the war lives
          deep in history,
seemingly overwhelmed
by stories.
        In this way

+

a virus hides in an urban
population,
          replicating itself before
breaking through.
              At first we're told we should avoid
crowds, we should wash
               our hands. In this way

+

the virus is an ancient story
changing itself all the time
              to suit its environment,
it is a dynamic story
            evolving to suit the genetic
complexities of its audience.

                                    In this way,
the Trojan War

+

lives deep in the cells of Greek literature,
and is also
                        transformative,
                                    so now
we are closing our schools,
we are shutting down
                                    the theater district.

In this way, crowds and transmission—
                                    the problem
with the metaphor implicit in this poem

+

is that the germ
                        of the Trojan War
helped the Greeks understand themselves,
and has helped me understand them,
                                    no matter
that the battle itself remains forever
                                    of small

+

historical importance.
                        A virus in the population
among, let's face it,
                        people I love
emerges to a vastly different result.

In this way, the germ of memory is not an actual
germ.
        In this way, the nurses

who might, for instance, tend to you
will adjust their masks
                    before they enter
your room.
            How are we doing today?
they'll ask, though they know
                        you might be dying.

+

Doing the best we can, I'm thinking,
                        here in the past,
looking out my window
                onto the dark street.

Extended Metaphor for Bad Government

When we found the shattered bottles in the freezer,
we picked the broken glass away
and ate the frozen wine.
                              Soon
we were drunk,

+

                    but we kept on eating
until I could barely stand,
and Jason, who was only nine,
                              laughed,
white wine dribbling down his chin.
Our father was far away
                    at his mysterious office.
The room spun

+

and when I leaned into the freezer
to search among the ice-cream bars
for another exploded bottle,
                              I heard
Jason cough—

a trickle of blood leaking from the corner
of his mouth

+

                    and he coughed again,
more blood,
                    and only then did we both realize
what had happened,

+

and what I remember most
is pressing paper towels
onto his lacerated tongue

as he cried quietly,
                            still quite drunk,
surrounded by wads of bloodied towels,
while I tried not to sway
                            or slur my words,
and, back from shopping,
                            our mother
pulled up in her black Honda.

+

And that night all I could think of
was the swallowed
                            sickle of glass
slicing up my brother's insides,
how more blood
was certainly pooling
                            somewhere
in the dark places.

The Last of Diocletian

Having ruled bloodlessly
                          for twenty years
the emperor retired
               Having survived his rule
the emperor became a farmer
                     Having successfully
retired
        he farmed cabbages   They were
beautiful cabbages
               They grew in martial rows
When the empire
             spiraled into war
the emperor barely noticed
                 Having spiraled into war
the people asked him
             to return
To be emperor again
               They were killing one another
They kept
         killing one another   If you could see
these beautiful cabbages
               he told them
you would never ask this of me
If you could see
            these purple cabbages
you would not ask me
              to water them
with your storms
            of insatiable greed
So said the emperor
              who having ruled well
retired to
         not exactly uselessness

Retired to awareness
                    of the chaos that always
follows the good days—
                    the destruction
of those he had loved
                    the wreckage of the state
Having ruled well
                    he died eventually
by his own hand
                    The bloodshed
continued
            Then a brief peace
Then war again
                    Back and forth it went   Centuries
of dead emperors
                    vanishing in the distance
Think of those rows
                    of perfect cabbages

My Jug of Poison

Fire ant colonies emerge most often after heavy rain.

The wet soil stimulates them to work, their mounds rising

and scarring the backyard, so what is there to do

but sprinkle them with poison

so they die quietly in their thousands? Then I go inside

and try not to think about it too much.

The same goes for the wasps' nests on the garage roof.

When I spray them, the wasps fall out like little black droplets

into the grass and when I know they are really dead,

I bat the nests down with a rake. It doesn't bother me

too much that they were crawling through dark burrows,

or whatever they're called, without knowing anything

about me, without even caring who I am.

Why should that matter? The flowers struggling to surprise me

say, *God bless you, Mr. President!*

with their vast colors and petals that flex in the wind.

They live in air and take an interest. *God bless you, too!*

I say to their ordered colorfulness—but did you know

there are vast populations completely unaware of me?

It is a sobering thought here on the back porch

with my jug of poison, looking over the yard

which was once a lot less beautiful than it is today.

Late Empires

A popular argument here in the academy
is that the Empire never fell.
Instead,
        it evolved into something new.

Thus,
      when we talk about
the late Empire period,
                    we are actually referring
to a brief expanse of time
within an endless process,

and not the beginning of an end.

For instance,
when I could no longer read the newspaper,
when it overwhelmed me
              completely,

I encountered a very old man
browsing the produce section
at the grocery store.

With one hand,
          he steadied himself
on his walker.

He held a pomegranate in the other,
examining it closely.

Is it wrong that, on seeing him,
my first thought was,
             Is this the state of my country?

In the parking lot,
my groceries were unusually heavy.

The empire
              felt tenuous.

The old man also
made his way across the pavement,
a bag of green apples
                        dangling from his walker.

The retirement home
yawned across the street.

In the academy
we have upended the notion that empires "fall,"
and who can blame us
                  for being afraid?

No one wants to die.

I loaded my groceries into the car.

For a moment, I could still see him
balancing on his walker,
                        the facility doors
sliding open.

FOUR

A Distant Row of Black Pines

When he was very drunk,
                                my father told me
how he had held another man's head underwater
until that man's entire body shuddered and relaxed
and only his leg
                                twitched on the muddy riverbank. *Anyway,*
he said,
                It was a long time ago. Time passes.
That's the thing about time.
                                        The bar was nearly empty.
For a long while he looked into the glittering
rows of bottles. *Drink up,*
                                he said at last,
fishing in his pocket for his keys.
                                        Drink up.

+

Is your fingernail
                part of your body,
the professor asked,
                                pretending to examine
the back of her perfectly manicured hand.

What about when you trim your fingernails?
Are the clippings part of your body?

I was watching very closely
as a fat black ant crawled across my open textbook.

What if they are false fingernails? What if your hand
is prosthetic? Are they part of you?

Are the microorganisms in your gut?

What I am trying to say, she said, *is that the borders*
of your body are not clear,
                    what I am trying to say
is that the moon is certainly not your body,
but the cellphone you're holding
is perhaps as much a part of your body as your fingernails,

and so she went on until class ended
and I closed my textbook
                    over the body of the ant.

+

There in the lecture hall,
my mind held an image of the moon,

but the moon kept flickering.

It would not hold its place.
It became something else,
                    a white face

in a receding patrol-car window
I remembered.
                    The moon, it turned out,

was not a part of my body,

though I could hold it in my thoughts
before it shifted,

though its likeness filled my mind

+

as mist might have filled a distant forest one evening
years ago,

my father rising from the riverbank
and disappearing, finally, into the black pines.

The mind rests there,
                    at the riverbank
where that body—it had been, in fact, a soldier—
has just stopped twitching,

+

                              or at that moment
when the professor told us our bodies
are merely relational, that they don't exist
beyond their *relations,*
                        in the same way that *car*
refers only to a complex relationship
between wheels, bumpers, engine, etc.

She was a thin woman, about forty,
black hair, bright red fingernails and lipstick.

My eyes lingered on her body as she spoke.

+

Your mother, he said,
                    is not going to be happy with us,
as he pulled from the parking lot
                              into the street.
The sodium lights glittered.
It had begun to rain. *I'm sorry*
about what I said back there.
                        It was all
bullshit. And he laughed. *I never killed*
anybody. The road was long and black.
He was talking about other things now,
some whore he met in Frankfurt,

                                        long before
I knew your mother.
                        Best part of the war.

+

The image of fingernail clippings
drifting to the floor.

The click of her heels as she walked from the podium.
A rustling of knapsacks.

My father didn't notice, at first, the blue lights,
the siren behind us.

+

                        Come on! he told
the cop who escorted him
to the patrol car,
                        I had two drinks! The cop,
surprisingly gentle, cuffed him and led him
away from me.
                        And then
she was helping my father's heavy body into the back seat,
closing the car door,
                        his moonlike face
pressed now to the window,
                                his breath fogging the glass,

+

an image that returns to me frequently,
the police car
                        pulling into the bodiless night, receding
while I stood for a moment
at the edge of the windy highway

and a distant row of black pines
swayed like a chorus.

Cannibalism

Several ancient skulls
                    unearthed in Ethiopia
with butchery marks around the eye sockets and occipital bones—

It's called "pot polishing"—a sign that bones have been boiled for
reasons of cookery—

+

I remember how the sun threw winter over you—

The cold light of Cleveland. The marble entry to the Museum of
          Natural History—

The exhibition was about Ethiopia—

Mandibles propped in plexiglass displays.
                              Incisors. Shinbone—

+

You were my father then. Now you are
                         in an urn—

The things we do: we remove the ring and the Timex and into a
          furnace with the rest—

Into the mouth
              goes the imagination. Into the gut—

+

You'd taken me to the museum because what else was there to do on
          a winter Sunday—

and now you wanted to get a drink somewhere—

The skulls in their cases like hunks of rock—

The great model ape-man crouched beside the carcass of an ancient yak—

+

When I heard you were finally dead
I could not understand how the world
                                    continued without you—

I fought traffic down Cedar Avenue
                            toward the hospital
where they'd stored your body—

The traffic just wouldn't move—

+

All my life, I had swallowed you
                            and now everything was jammed up
on East Boulevard—

The trees glittered meanly in their skins of ice—

And there was the Museum of Natural History crouched in the snow
like a cold fact—

The Time Machine

If you insist
          that reading great literature
is like bringing a time-traveler
into conversation with you,

then you will likely find that traveler burdened
with old-fashioned prejudices,

+

but if you imagine, instead, that *you,* the reader,
are the time-traveler
                    traveling to an era you never
experienced,
          standing among ancient people
on temple stairs, a little lost, bewildered—

+

or so the old man thought,
two days before he was to retire,

having encountered one more student
who wouldn't read another page
of patriarchal, colonialist
                bullshit,

snow piling up on his office windowsill,
                    the ticking
of sleet on glass,
          holding a book he'd discovered
on his shelf,
          a book he'd last read
as a youth, *Life in Ancient Rome*—

+

The sound of that student's heels
as she left the lecture hall,

           thoughtless
and fierce,

      out into winter sunlight.
What was her name? He couldn't

           remember—

+

The snow-filled yards that stretched below,
the white of open pages in his hands,

           tracks
of black gravel peeking through where snow
swept over a driveway,

       his father, one evening years ago,
tracking snow into the hallway,

+

shaking snow off his jacket onto the carpet,
Don't wanna spend all day reading, kid,

         he'd said,
that'll turn you into a faggot for sure.
So he'd put *Life in Ancient Rome* facedown
on the kitchen table

     and smiled.
He was thirteen

     and he loved his father—

+

Students congregating around the campus fountain
or in parking lots,

     staring into their phones—

what did any of them know of history

or time?

+

Later that evening, after they'd
shoveled the snow away,

as dark came down on the city,
after his mother put fish sticks in the oven,
when the house was quiet,

he read about the practice
among Romans

of offering philosophical observations
on tombstones,

+

Here lies Publius Orfius
who now knows better than you
that after death there is no ferryman, no Lethe,
no three-headed dog,

there is only soil
and bones. Think of that, traveler

+

and rest a moment here—

+

That'll turn you into a faggot for sure.

They'd laughed at that,
he and his father, sitting at the dining-room table
that evening

waterproofing boots for Saturday's chores,

while his mother talked with her sister on the phone
and a dog barked from down the black road

by the cemetery,

+

the campus grown silent,
night coming on,
                        roads closing from the storm,
and here he was, a childless old man
                              among dusty books
in a half-empty office,
                        the future having come for him at last—

+

But who would teach about the Romans now?
Eight hundred years of Romans
                              stretching their legs
among sun-dappled temples
talking about chariot races.
                        Who would speak for them?

+

Romans among the heat-blasted
                        arches,
Romans in their great apartment blocks,
                              gladiatorial,
purple robed,
            among amphorae at the sunlit shipyards—
how he'd traveled back to them,
                        with his flashlight
that night
            under the covers—

+

The office quiet now,
                  the janitors gone home

to their families,
                    every office but his
dark, the hallways dark—

+

For now, he'd leave the boxed-up books
                              on his desk,
he'd close the door.
                    He'd walk the parking lot
through a confusion
                    of snow
to his snowcapped car.
                    He'd drive slowly
through the onrush of snow,
                    back to the empty house
where his history was.

Absences

She sometimes discovered letters
                                    her husband had written to her
during his last weeks
                        hidden where he must have known
she'd eventually find them.
                            At first, these delighted her
because she could hear his voice in them,
                                            his dry wit
and intelligence,
                    his observations about their years together,
about getting sick.

+

                        As time went on, she told me,
she came to dread opening an old cookbook
or little-used drawer,
                        knowing that to do so was to invite him
too forcefully back into her life.
                                That is, she came to value
his memory without necessarily
                                wanting to encounter him again.
It was good, therefore,
                        that as the years passed
these discoveries occurred more infrequently
and eventually stopped.

+

                        She said she often wondered
why he'd done it.
                    He had been a playful man, a man
who loved the attention of others,
                                which he courted

with grace and skill.
                    Had he been unable to bear
the vast inattention
                    death eventually would bring?
Or had he intended to let her release him slowly,
to mute,
          for her,
                    the finality of his absence?

+

Would it be fair to say that,
                    as long as a letter
might remain
               hidden in a never-used vase,
he was still somehow alive,
                    able to reveal himself
to her,
          to offer up a memory
or surprising thought?
                    No, it was not fair to say that,
she told me,
               closing her book and taking the cup of cold coffee
to the sink.
          It was not fair to say anything like that.

+

Outside, it had grown cold
                    and frost made circuitry
on the windows.
               It had long ago become possible for her to tell me
how maddening he had been,
                    and to laugh. He had been,
she now understood,
                    deeply flawed, imperious, obsessed

with his legacy,
                    and she didn't miss that part of him.
Outside, a row of blackbirds
                          descended from the power line
into the snow.
                    She asked me if I'd seen her keys.

+

The world is a vast and lonely place.
                                Death is vaster still,
and inconceivably silent.
                          Every word I write is an effort
to preserve the intricacy of my own mind
                                  against the eventual
certainty of my absence.
                    This is the context for my poems,
an elaborate set within which my actors
                                speak their lines.

+

That said,
          I helped her put on her winter coat
and watched her hurry to her car, where she brushed the windows
clear of snow.
                    How good it feels to be alive, snow
sticking to one's hair,
                    cold air in the throat.
She eased the car from the curb,
                                turned left onto Twelfth Street,
and drove out of my poem.

+

It may be that a couple more letters remain,
pressed between the pages of books

she will never read,
                    silenced and pointless.
One day, a stranger might find in one
                              a conversation piece.
That is not for me to say,
                    up too late,
writing this story
                    about absence, forgetting,
and the conceits of authors.

Anesthesia

I felt her push the needle in,
$\qquad\qquad$ then nothing,
a void where the hospital room had been,
and when I finally woke
$\qquad\qquad\qquad$ it was early evening. The room
was different,
$\qquad\qquad$ smaller. It was a different
room. Light angled in
from a courtyard,
$\qquad\qquad$ gray-gold winter light,

+

and I could hear the nurses
$\qquad\qquad\qquad$ in the hall—
incoherent
$\qquad\qquad$ conversation through the walls.
The food cart's rattle.
$\qquad\qquad\qquad$ I was thinking
about the moment the needle pierced my skin,

+

and then what?
$\qquad\qquad$ I reached for a word,
blackness,
$\qquad\qquad$ but that wasn't it. The anesthetic
was more
$\qquad\qquad$ self-canceling than blackness,
within which one might
$\qquad\qquad\qquad$ live and think.

+

I suppose I was like one of those summerhouses
during the off-season.

All my windows were black.

On the back deck,
                    behind the covered pool,
snow decorated a row of garbage cans.
Silence, silence.
                    Still, behind the Sheetrock,
the wires were alive.
                    The furnace kicked on
to keep the pipes from freezing.

+

A zero, an absence of time
or narrative.
                    A deleted file.
                              I'd told myself
I wanted to get
                    to nothing,
and here it was, and it was
                              less than fleeting,

+

and when it was over
I was glad to be alive.
                    Winter light
through hospital windows,
the nurse
          adjusting tubes. *I see you've come around,*
she'd said, smiling down at me.

Casual snow against the window.

+

In the courtyard
                children threw snow
at one another.
               Their voices
echoed up the hospital walls.
                     Every minute
the light got less golden.
               Soon, they would
have to go home to dinner.
                 I'll never
escape myself.

Automotive

I keep returning to the image of a kitten
asleep in the engine

as a way of understanding
the history of my country.

So warm under the car's hood,
the hidden sweetness in the dark machinery.

+

Start the car.

+

[The sound the kitten makes.]

+

Happy slaves on a lazy afternoon
sleeping in the shadow of hay bales.

A banjo lying in the sun.
Stolen apples.

A lithograph on the wall in my father's office:
The sweet ol' summuh time.

+

My mother bought me a kitten.
I brought it home in a cardboard box
and how I loved that kitten,
the way it purred in my arms
and pressed its cold, wet nose against my cheek.

+

Start the car.

+

In a poem by Jorie Graham,
history is a hand grenade lodged in the pulp of a young tree.
The tree grows, the tree grows.

One day, a farmer chops it down for firewood, burns it.
Imagine his surprise when the grenade—

+

[The sound the kitten made.]

+

My mother promised me a kitten,
but it escaped,

scurrying into the distant past.

+

I used to think history moved inexorably forward
from villainy into truth,

but the kitten was nowhere to be seen.
I stood on the porch and called into the wind.

Only the car cooled in the driveway,
its engine ticking.

+

All those kittens asleep by the hay bales—
they had had too much to eat,

and now they wanted a warm place to relax.

The sun bore down upon them.

+

The grenade explodes as resentment, as rage,
as the final expression

of unredressed wrong.

When the kitten licked my ear
I laughed and fed it treats.

+

Start the car.

+

What did I know of evil?

My father worked long evenings in his study
so I could go to school.

I had a safe childhood. Don't make me feel guilty
about that.

I'm not guilty of anything here.

+

[That sound.]

+

They had stolen the apples and the time,
but in the distance you could see

their master walking from the barn,
scowling—

Lazy, lazy. Oh, you lazy . . .

+

Anyway, I loved that kitten
and when I couldn't find it,
I panicked

not because it was a metaphor for the history of my country

but because I loved its little pink tongue,
the way it washed its paws—

+

The engraving hung upstairs, in his study.

In the early evenings, the sunlight hit it,
a bright red square

before I was born.

+

The grenade keeps exploding
into my adulthood.

+

I'm just going to run to the store for groceries,
my mother said.

You kids behave.
You kids be good until I get back.

Its little pink tongue. Its cold nose.

The jangle of car keys.

ABOUT THE AUTHOR

Kevin Prufer is the author of several poetry collections, among them *National Anthem* (2008), *In a Beautiful Country* (2011), *Churches* (2014), *How He Loved Them* (2018), and *The Art of Fiction* (2021). His work has been short-listed for the Rilke Prize, long-listed for the Pulitzer Prize, and named in the best-of-the-year lists from *The New York Times Book Review, Publishers Weekly,* and others. Prufer teaches in the Creative Writing Program at the University of Houston and in the low-residency Creative Writing MFA program at Lesley University.

Poetry is vital to language and living. Since 1972, Copper Canyon Press has published extraordinary poetry from around the world to engage the imaginations and intellects of readers, writers, booksellers, librarians, teachers, students, and donors.

WE ARE GRATEFUL FOR THE MAJOR SUPPORT PROVIDED BY:

academy of american poets

THE PAUL G. ALLEN FAMILY FOUNDATION

POETRY FOUNDATION

CULTURE

Lannan

the point
envision·enact·evolve

ART WORKS. National Endowment for the Arts arts.gov

WASHINGTON STATE ARTS COMMISSION

A&
OFFICE OF ARTS & CULTURE
SEATTLE

The Witter Bynner Foundation for Poetry

TO LEARN MORE ABOUT UNDERWRITING
COPPER CANYON PRESS TITLES,
PLEASE CALL 360-385-4925 EXT. 103

WE ARE GRATEFUL FOR THE MAJOR SUPPORT PROVIDED BY:

Richard Andrews and
  Colleen Chartier
Anonymous
Jill Baker and Jeffrey Bishop
Anne and Geoffrey Barker
Donna Bellew
Will Blythe
John Branch
Diana Broze
John R. Cahill
Sarah Cavanaugh
Keith Cowan and Linda Walsh
Stephanie Ellis-Smith and
  Douglas Smith
Mimi Gardner Gates
Gull Industries Inc.
  on behalf of William True
William R. Hearst III
Carolyn and Robert Hedin
David and Jane Hibbard
Bruce S. Kahn
Phil Kovacevich and Eric Wechsler

Lakeside Industries Inc.
  on behalf of Jeanne Marie Lee
Maureen Lee and Mark Busto
Ellie Mathews and Carl Youngmann
  as The North Press
Larry Mawby and Lois Bahle
Hank and Liesel Meijer
Petunia Charitable Fund and
  adviser Elizabeth Hebert
Madelyn S. Pitts
Suzanne Rapp and Mark Hamilton
Adam and Lynn Rauch
Emily and Dan Raymond
Joseph C. Roberts
Cynthia Sears
Kim and Jeff Seely
D.D. Wigley
Barbara and Charles Wright
In honor of C.D. Wright,
  from Forrest Gander
Caleb Young as C. Young Creative
The dedicated interns and faithful
  volunteers of Copper Canyon Press

The pressmark for Copper Canyon Press
suggests entrance, connection, and interaction
while holding at its center
an attentive, dynamic space for poetry.

This book is set in PT Serif Pro.
Book design by Phil Kovacevich.
Printed on archival-quality paper.